T0168652

dark thirty

Volume 65

Sun Tracks

An American Indian Literary Series

Series Editor

Ofelia Zepeda

Editorial Committee

Larry Evers

Joy Harjo

Geary Hobson

N. Scott Momaday

Irvin Morris

Simon J. Ortiz

Kate Shanley

Leslie Marmon Silko

Luci Tapahonso

dark thirty

Santee Frazier

The University of Arizona Press

Tucson

The University of Arizona Press

© 2009 Santee Frazier

All rights reserved

www.uapress.arizona.edu

Library of Congress Cataloging-in-Publication Data

appear on the last printed page of this book.

Publication of this book is made possible in part by the proceeds of a permanent endowment
created with the assistance of a Challenge Grant from the National Endowment for the
Humanities, a federal agency.

Manufactured in the United States of America on acid-free, archival-quality paper.

To the memory of my grandfather

Ralph England

And I thought in awe of her,—she who had slept with Death to tear a man-child from underneath her heart, while I was unconsciously wandering.

—W.E.B. DuBois, "Of the Passing of the First Born"

contents

Jack Move

Aerosol

dark thirty

Root Juice

He walks out of the junkyard,

    like an oar, the root juice in his clutches.

No wrapper on that 2-liter—

    the undulating root gathering at the cap.

This ancient thing in plastic,

    plucked from the dirt and given the means to heal.

This tincture of the gully bend—

    that ends gossip and calls down a flood.

No hymn or myth tells how this root grows,

    a conjure pickled in a brine of spit and corn.

He stops, slams the juice on the hood—

    loosens the cap and tightens his mouth for a drink.

Dry Creek

Mama's Work

Mama tucked the coffee can between her wrist and hip

and walked down Dry Creek Road. Her eyes lined-up,

blush and lipstick, her Levi's shorts cut above the thigh.

And what it was to see those farmers cutting down wheat,

side-glancing mama, barefoot and brown. Sometimes it's flour,

sometimes money when she empties the can. Her work

in the quiet corners of barns on the hay, on hot days

when locusts launch themselves out of thickets.

I stare down Dry Creek Road looking for her wrist and hip,

her splayed hair and small toes walking out of a pone-colored dust.

Chauncey

There ain't no since starin intah that eye,
dead as can be, stabbed with a fork or sumthin.

Dang near had tah pluck my yard bird
other day, we had done ate all are fatback.

Meely over tah tha Teller's Liquor got caught
round back drankin listo, huffin on some gold.

Heard Joe Bunch's retarded boy don't do anythang
but sit in tires and read nudie books.

How come you ain't usin no grease,
dem taters gon have no dang flavor?

Thelma ain't got long I heard, she was gettin skinny,
turnin all yella, they feedin her threw a tube too.

Deanie is supposed tah get thrown in for burnin
that ol Nakedhead boy down over tah Barren Fork.

They said ol Caroline was moppin the floor,
usin gas, guess she caught farer, burned her leags good.

Calvin can barely keep them dentures in is jaw,
every time he talks, he's ah chewing like a horse.

I told you I cain't go nowhere yet, Elbert gon tah take
me bingo, it's Winsdee when all em old ladies at worship.

First time I drank listo we was over in Eldon,

hungover like deer meat, just ah sweatin.

By god, I'd kick the ceilin if I won'ted to, hell

I took Karate for bout five years from Marty Jumper.

Nick Cheater's good with them dodges, he just ah

wrenches them thangs like they was his wiener or sumthin.

Hunter's Moon

My legs catching
the brush, mama's hand
    on the nape of my neck—
beyond her shoulder,
    the trailer shrinking
in the night.
     We hunker down by an oak,
        under the hunter's moon,

    among the sprawling
shadows of branches—
    we could disappear, she says,
stay hidden in these trees.
    Even this far down the hill
I can see him in the window,
    reaching back,
        dealing out the beating

    the length of the trailer
until it reaches the bedroom.
    It has been going on
for years, my mother, her mother,
    sisters, whoever was left born
into this rage who did not run
    into the night as we have.
       Still we plan to return,

    when the dawn sends
its icy rays across these hills,
    or the flitting light
of the sheriff stops
    at our trailer.
She lowers me down
    to the gravel road,
       and we trudge uphill—

the trailer still lit.
He must have fallen asleep
     by now, she says, and turns
the knob: my grandma and grandpa,
     lying there naked,
as if they'd been flung
     on the bed. When they wake,
          I will forget about leaving.

Joe Bunch

Grape dumplins, skillet bread,
wild onions, pinto beans,
    nuthin like lard tah make em better.

Gimme those dang nitro pills,
mah heart's actin up and I need tah
    clear mah arteries for I eat that fatback.

Talk in mah good ear, got earaches
when I was a youngun still, and
    mama poured hot baby oil down it.

Member that time I got stuck
in that pile of tires
    lookin fur that dang ol possum?

I didn't even know my hand
was a cookin on the stove like at,
    thank my nerve endin's dyin on me again.

By god, I'm gon haul off
and hit cha if you keep
    knockin my cane over like at!

Boy pull them britches up,
nobody wonts tah
    see them ol stink cheeks ah yours!

Check that bathroom for Chauncey,
prawlly locked himself
    in there drankin all my smell-good.

I heard that Hammer boy
cut that one Procter girl up,
    he liked to have killt her wit that buck blade.

Bluetop

Her head bangs against the window
and dash when I stop and turn,
my legs too short to work
the brakes.

      Mama's crooked
brow, her makeup smearing away,
slurs something about good
ol' boy music, a pint of Kentucky
Deluxe in her hand. Two hours,
she said, and three days later,
Tuesday, she is finally wanting
to stop. I am getting better
at the turns, guiding her
Cutlass through these hills,
ten miles an hour, gravel roads,
the Cutlass

         rattling out the last
fumes of gas. Engine stops,
the night dimly lit by the moon
hung over the treetops;
owls calling each other from
hilltop to valley bend.

          The radio
fades in and out of static,
tractors revving, cows lowing,
and we may never make it back,
home still five hills away, daylight
coming over rocky edges of the hills.

Nick Cheater

I done dropped that tranny,
      wrenched on that thang least till supper time,

didn't have no luck neither.
      Hell, that ratchet set I had was slippery as a dang ol perch.

Was up in grease tah my ears
      that one day I was rippin the engine block out mah Trans Am.

Ain't seen that ol station wagon
      yah had, that ol burgundy one with gold trim.

You reckon that Buick up dah road
      is fur sale still? I thank he ought to let it go for bout

seven, eight hunderd, shit,
      last I shot-the-shit with him, he told me 750 and one ah mah dogs.

Your car still make that funny noise
      when you rev up in the mornins? You might need tah get

your intake checked, hell,
      your head gasket might even be makin you car sound like at.

Told yah not tah get your car fixed in town,
      they thank since they got all em machines they know everythang.

Ol Marty Jumper took his Chevy
      over tah Good Wrench, they charged him double I woulda.

Baptism of the Knife

Circus Fire

Ringmaster makes freak show of Mangled and his face, a bean juice–colored boy
     whose ancestry
and tongue have passed into the void of circus blurb, verbatim of sideshow,
     squawk of his primitive origins.

The audience calls him to dance for the accordion, *set him on fire*, they say, *make his*
     feet shuffle,
make him say circus words. Flail that whip; make him jump through the fire-hoop!

This is his execution, this is when the Ringmaster points the six-shot Saturday night
     special.
No dying that he asks for, no racket-cum-utter from his mouth but taught schema;
     the noun,
the tree, logic of the already, his origins in circus books bound.

Mangled mounts a speckled horse in a studded taco-hat and chaps, the lasso-artist,
     the spoof,
tossing daggers at full gallop is his trade.
The plainsman, wrangler of women and kids, the inmate, con man—breaking ankles,
     dribbling the rock—
lyricist of the corner, drunkard of dive bars, prison-shank assassin, pusher-man,
     alien.

Mangled makes tum-tum on the skin of a drum, listen to him sing, tum-tum,
     Ringmaster states as matter-of-fact,
like a foreman says to Dew Boss: *my pickers have picked enough tobacco, and my cane*
     choppers
have chopped enough cane, they worked through lashings of whip and rain.

The Bottle collector

Young Mangled stuffed cheese sandwiches in his britches, ate them at the creek—a wash, the concrete sewer bed. Mangled's momma locked him out of the house in the summers, so Mangled would not see the musky men who came for his mother—the plank-floor seductress, clack of her heels, her taut, sweaty thighs, the musky smell of fuck. He roamed the uncitied dirt between the streets and yards, collecting pop bottles, beer bottles, and shiny metal he sold for popgun money, glue, and the occasional haircut. Sometimes, when he got home at dark, dirt-faced, barefoot, and ashy, he would find his momma passed out on the pink divan, snoring.

Baptism of the Knife

Unsheathed on a creek stone, it was rusting at the handle and caked with scales. Mangled took it by the rust, raised the blade to his face, flies still huddling on the remnants of guts and gill on the long, curved blade. Sun-perch smelled up the bank, and creek bugs scooted in and out of the bright-spark current. Mangled dipped the knife in the creek, and as he turned the flat of the blade toward his eyes, the glue haze faded to white, and there it was, the flitting blade in the dark.

Glue and Knives

Young Mangled liked the starry gaze, dust sparks, the floating midmorning dust. Paper-bagged glue huffer. Mangled's memory deaf with glue. The creek-bed boy, bean juiced and ashy, huffed the glue until his eyes glazed over, hazy lost in a damp brain, gaze empty as tin. *Goo*, he called it, his lost L's, the slur of huff. *Goo* and knife, tossing knives into tree trunks, took aim, tip and handle—he aimed well, tossing knives in the thicket.

Fragments

smell of kitchen
        burnt bread
taters frying
        thumping the grease

                hands mimic
a bird
                behind locked
                thumbs
the sun

skillet face
                slit eyes
bullish nose
                pursed
                lips
grit of teeth
                he is five or six

hair a matted nest
                head
big for his body

cheekbones
                greasy
shining face wide like
                like bark
                        etched

The carnival

Pickax

It all started with a nudge, a jab to the mouth,
$\qquad$a bat, a hammer, sending her over the kitchen
table, to the floor, through the bedroom door.
$\qquad$With one swift blow, he sank into her shoulder.

The pickax, rusty, frail at the handle,
$\qquad$dug deep in her. Taters frying, door swung
open, locusts still buzzing in the dusk.
$\qquad$Some man I'd never met, snarling at her,

trying to lift the ax out of his handiwork,
$\qquad$to raise it once more, and this time not miss.
The same woman that bore me from her fifteen-
$\qquad$year-old hips sprawled out on the linoleum,

the same woman who held a warm towel
$\qquad$to my earache, when all I could do was cry,
thought of me, once, when she feared her life
$\qquad$would pass. The last time it was a knife in her thigh

while she gazed at the television, smoking
$\qquad$a Salem, unaware he had unsheathed the buck-
blade from his hip, wanting to splay her
$\qquad$like a white-tailed doe hung up by the hooves,

still steaming in the knee-deep winter.
$\qquad$Yet I knew him, his muzzle-loader, that sweet
woo on the hay, as she tells it, the summer-lit barn,
$\qquad$her hips shrugging her jeans loose, for the first time,

on the barn floor. She remembers that I was the coming

months, the winter baby, hung low on her torso.

Plunk of grease, clink of glass, the passing dusk,

and the pickax will not budge. The living room flung

apart, crooked. His shoulders tensing for one last pull

of the ax. A deep summer gust from the south

carrying the smell of bait, of nightcrawlers and crawdads

rotting on the gully bank. *How else could you have ended up?*

he asks, standing over her, dust of flour on her thighs,

biscuit dough stuck to her fingers, the dark coming,

moths gathering on the porch, lit dim yellow,

his foot on her shoulder, wriggling the ax until it slips free.

Nauxcey Moss

e tolt me
      it weren't gon
hurt like at
on dah porch
      and I aim
dah gun
with mah
      armpit shot
dem yard birds
      like deys fur
eatin I ran off
passed dah
      thicket I
ain't herd
nuthin ain't herd
      gramma yellin
bout dose
      chickens mah
ear was thick
mah ed numb
      face ringin
like taters
in dere
      all dem
noises sounds
      olt like dey
down yonder
like dere's
      whole lot

ah wind
in mah ed
      some ah
dem birds
      weren't dead
jus layin
dere bleeden
      sick on dey
own blood
gramma look
      in mah ear
Bluerock look
      in mah ear
dey blew in
it dey pour
      wax in it
but it still
      thick still
ringin
      gramma fry
up dem chickens
      gizzards and all
fur supper

Gunshot Conjure

Down past Stilwell
        on gravel roads
    that wind through the guts
of Adair County,
    into hills, red, yellow,
        whatever color
    autumn is—trailers
on the hillsides
    or in valley bends,
        avocado-green, sky-blue,
    whatever color trailers are—
grandpa drove,
    until all I could see
        was sycamore and oak
    fog-thick in every direction
but up. He guided
    the '78 Thunderbird
        down Wahilla Road,
    under the hardwoods
where Bluerock's
    trailer sat—Bluerock, root-juice
        healer, who could gaze
    into woodstove fires
and conjure the end
    of nightmares,
        arthritis. As frost
    melted away from the grass,
I waited in the car,
    wondering what fire

or root cures rage

in a man's soil-worn hands.

How Bluerock got the root

in the jug was anyone's

guess. Was it grown

in the jug's belly?

Snakeroot, bloodroot

floating in juice

like river-grown thickets,

gnarling themselves

up through the surface

current. Grandpa

cried in that trailer,

on his knees, not remembering

how he choked or shoved,

kicked or whipped,

just begging

for the root once more.

Late one night Grandpa

lay out on the gravel yard,

groaning, the buckshot

speckling his forearm,

then into his chest,

grandma standing behind

the four-ten shotgun,

her shirt ripped at the collar.

From the porch door

beside her hip, elbows out,

hands pressed to my ears,

I winced for rifle's

next boom. Grandpa's

chest became myth,

a drunk-angered slur

on his wheelchair—

hands, once so large,

shrinking to bone

and yellow at the knuckle,

gripping the Old Weller

by the neck. She wheeled

him to bed, laid

him under the covers

as he cried and yelled

in her face, just as she

must have done for me

when I cut my first teeth,

rubbing my gums with a cube

of ice to numb me to sleep.

One-Room Apartment

1

I watch them moan
     and cringe—fastening
themselves together
on the queen-size bed
     that fills up most of our
one-room apartment.
Their bodies dank,
rattling the bed.
     Old Milwaukee cans,
tall, glinting, 5:13, 5:13
     on the clock I watch
and watch. Passed-out,
sprawled on the bed,
     snoring. What sound
could wake her?
The crush of cans,
slamming doors, fists
     on skin, the rattling
bed. 5:13, 5:13, the sun
     came and went. Snoring
and snoring. Their mouths
bellowing steam, soot,
     fumes from their innards.
I wait for her soft, round
toes to stir,
for her to wake and see
     me here on the couch,
not knowing that I had

seen her face riled, lit
in the early sun as she
arched her back, restless,
    5:13, moaning
herself to sleep. 5:13,
gussying herself up,
blow-dryer in one hand,
    beer in the other.

Z

I search the cabinet
    and icebox—licked
peanut butter from
a knife. Wild onions,
    dank with mold,
unraveling at the bulb.
I search the cabinet,
and icebox—A-1
    and stale saltines.
The blackberries, dry,
    shrinking, soft, wrinkled
like wet skin. I search
the cabinet and icebox—
    drink the pickle juice
from the jar. Bologna,
hard at the edges,
browning on the kitchen
    table since yesterday.
I search the cabinet
    and icebox—the curdling
milk almost smells drinkable.

The Carnival

I studied every ride on the midway—
watched them groan, twirling
    light into blur, the Ferris wheel's

last passengers pointing out
    from their seats to town's end.
These monuments that have risen

    between the hills, to be forgotten
as the lights go out. Where was she
    in this hazy night? Maybe half-lit

in Red-Oak Bar, leaning on a man,
    wedged between his thighs. I wonder
what it is to dream of autumn,

    balled up on a park bench,
the tilt-a-whirl in my gaze,
    wanting a passing car to take me to her.

Among these monuments I am too
    small to find my way to the sandbanks
where she sometimes takes a man,

    where sometimes I wander,
skipping stones, while she earns
    in the backseat of a car or under

a gun rack. It is hours like these
    you learn the path of a ditch—a quiet
only the huffers know. Day breaks:

    the carnies have loaded up the rides,
heading out of town in a convoy,
    leaving nothing behind, not even the grass.

Skillet Face

Mangled and Beautiful Girls

Mangled's skillet face and slit eyes made it hard to meet beautiful women. No one wants to mate with a skillet face; bean juice, in his day, was too dark. All those pinup queens, pop-bottle legstresses on the soda-pop signs were sheriff's daughters, the kind the preachers coveted, the All-American prize, the Midwest beauty queen. He got to mate when he had the change, rented rooms by the hour, and got off in alleys.

Ripped On a Friday Night

Mangled went to jail for cutting a man across the face in Tuxy's Bar one Friday night. The judge gave him a year in the county jail. Last time he got thrown in jail, the guards stole his money when they booked him, so he took his last hundred-dollar bill and folded it and stuck it in his mouth where a tooth had once been. After a year, Mangled got released, took the money out of his mouth, and walked back into Tuxy's.

county Jail

Mangled stuffed boiled eggs in his pockets while he was on mess duty in the county jail, and when he went back to his cell, he pulled them out and ate them, yolk and all, with salt. He had pictures taped on his wall of bathing suit pinups on the beach drinking Dr. Pepper. His bed was a mat on a steel sheet bolted to the wall, and his blanket was itchy gray. When the lights went out, he'd stare at the ceiling, wriggling one of his front teeth that was knocked loose in a tussle over a candy bar. His cell stank of boiled-egg fart and cement, and just before he dozed off, Mangled would practice his throws, imagining the blade shiny with a sharp edge.

Ringmaster

One payday the circus was in town, and Mangled wanted to see all those strange animals people say they have at circuses. When he walked into the big top, he saw the clowns driving around in their beep-beep cars, making balloons. He saw people flying around on ropes way up toward the top of the tent. He knew then he wanted to throw knives, throw them at the show women in the sparkling clothes. The next day, out in the pasture, the big top now packed away, the crew hitching the trailers. Mangled threw his knives for Ringmaster, hitting targets in one, two, three spins of the blade. Mangled left town with two dollars in his sock and a pint of whiskey in his back pocket for a life in the circus.

Mangled, Letters, and the Target Girl

Only to hoot, to speak flitting blade in the dark, mouth
able to sound verb for thing, him chicken eat. Not know
gallop but for sound, stud but for knotting haunches,
tipping its body, arching its head toward dirt. Chewing
hay under a ranch hat, bean-juice skin tight as saddle
leather, neck stiff as a coffee can—as lanterns go out,
stud fed and tied to post—Mangled piles up some hay,
rests his bones for the long day of pounding tent stakes.

———

Ringmaster swigs moonshine from jar, stomps camp,
looking for LuLu's pudgy round face. Mangled wakes,
remembers the switching, musky soil, the stud's hooves
sucking mud, LuLu moaning in the night. Stock of spade,
thud of stakes drove in the dirt; the performers sagging
in their bones, their breath spent breaking in frost-thick
dawn, the trees swaying barer as the day wears on, wind
carrying the red and yellow leaves across the fields. After
the act, LuLu writes letters for Mangled, that he trots
stud into the show, bullwhip in one hand, bridle the other.

———

She did not write about a scar that runs down his cheek,
or the clown he stabbed near Tulsa. LuLu writes about
his new square-toed boots and the creased-up Levi's he
bought at a mercantile in Lawrence, Kansas. She writes
about his haircuts, how if he could, he would write letters
himself, but signed with his throwing hand. Sometimes she
reads him Westerns and Sgt. Rock comic books—she lies
about what the stories say—that his skillet face ain't so flat.

———

Him horse ride, LuLu throw with knife, fire cook meat. Him
audience laugh make, headdress wear. Him horse smell
snout, hooves scrape rock out, horse-apple chew hand.

———

Sundays LuLu and Mangled go to the Baptist church before the start
of the show. They sing hymns, sometimes they walk down
to the river with the congregation and watch the preacher dunk
the pudgy babies into the bright-sparked current, Mangled
thinks about the creek-bed soil, LuLu in her Sunday dress,
her face painted blush, lips bright, glossy, shined for the show.

Mangled and the Adventures of Sgt. Rock

Bloused boots, bayonets, pistol smoke.
Mangled thumbs the cartoons drawn
in the book: grunts hill humping, Sgt.
Rock busting his Colt .45, .50-caliber
shells hung from his shoulders. LuLu
reads bubbles and squares, each word
called a name. Mangled thinks his boots,
scuffed square-toe, need polishing, a spit
shine with his sock and elbow, shiny
as brown can shine. Flutter of moths
in the lantern light. LuLu moves her lips
like she does during the act, red apple
atop her head, waiting for the flung blade.
As she reads, Mangled smells his armpits,
scratches his head, and sounds words
as she reads them in syllables. Mangled
thinks of the drawing, how drawing can
make words, how words make sound,
how stab make knife, knife make shine.

Mangled, the Knife, and the Funeral

Mangled stood up in his best boots and creased black britches and sang church hymns about the cross and salvation. *Glory be the name o'lord.* He listened to the Bible man holler up the good news: Father, Son, Holy Spirit can save you from the fire. Mangled wanted to bury his favorite knife with her, lay it in her casket, the blade that he threw around at the creek, at the targets he made out of beer boxes and roadkill. But he kept it in his boot, and after he poured his handful of dirt over her casket, he walked off, as did many men that came to the service that day.

Mangled in the Sunset

Mangled decides to quit the circus—his arms have grown tired, a few daggers have slipped, and the horse he once rode round the arena—in its regalia, in all its studded glory—lay dead a few weeks back, gone gimp on a jump and shot through the skull by Ringmaster. Mangled buried it in the dirt they were camping on. Mangled remembers his trot, the stutter gallop, and those falling balloons, all the reds and blues, the gazing townsfolk gazing at his trade, steering the stud right. But Mangled's stud was dead; all the brown of him would never touch his brown again. And Mangled walks away from the circus, never had nothing but the clothes on his back.

Odd Jobs

38-year-old fry cook. Dishwasher. Motel-room cleaner. Car-part ripper. Fabric presser. Chicken catcher. Had a pretty good job as a maintenance man; got free rent on a furnished one-room— white walls, a bed, a shower, a droopy, shit-green chair. Sometimes Mangled hung his laundry around the room after he washed it in the bathtub. Mangled liked to fix pipes and repair drywall, but a man like him could not stay working. He liked whiskey early mornings; sometimes drank mint listo to take the edge off.

Mangled, Memory, and the Wheelchair

All of him wants to go back to the circus—the
gun smoke, whinny of his stud, the Ringmaster's
sleek mustache salt and pepper on his lip—but
there is his footless leg, stroke-face sagging off
his skull. His slit eyes dark as prunes, and his
footless leg a dangling, sock-clad nub—with his
foot had gone the square-toed boots, the spurs;
the foot now just air, a list of cities, shows,
trained animals. White hospital gown, sock nub,
bedpan, watery gaze of death, ashy elbows and
knees. Bean-juiced, shriveled Mangled on the
wheelchair.

Jack Move

Firecracker

A row of glistening kids stood under the pool lamp, gazing through the fence links as one of the witnesses, beer coolie in one hand, flyswatter in the other, reported to the cops that the guilty boys had scattered.

I saw them, belly first, feet slapping the sidewalk, running through the breezeway. And when the cops, in their shiny tactical boots, knocked at my apartment, asking what I saw, I told them the kid's name was Paul, that he was dribbling down the breezeway when the M-80 went off in his face, that earlier in the day, over by the dumpster, the same boys were stuffing Ladyfingers in a calico's mouth.

Later that night the blasters blared cassettes of the latest turntable mixes spun by Miguel from 7-B, and those who could danced on the cardboard, locking their joints, contorting their bodies until they broke into a fluid sequence of acrobatic movements.

Coin Laundry

Spinning washers. Whirr of dryers. Soda machine humming.
Baskets on hips, underneath chairs and tables. The infant
boy or girl, head on its mother's chest, cradled by the nape.
The mother ties knots on each shoulder, strapping the infant to her,
in a carrier too rough-hewn and tattered to have been store bought.
On the edge of sleep, gnawing at its knuckle, the infant
must be teething, crying in the early morning hours when the darkness
is thinning, the sky dim as shade. She puts a slice of orange
to its mouth; the infant refuses and looks to her other shoulder.
Its thin hair, light brown, undulating, through and around
its mother's long, wood-brown fingers. Until that one last coo,
the coo of sleep, the light push of the infant's chest.
Spinning washers. Whirr of dryers. Soda machine humming.
Baskets on hips, underneath chairs and tables. The infant
boy or girl, still sleeping, ear over the mother's heart
as if still in the womb, kicks once, twice. Pre-wash and spin.
Wash and spin. Rinse and spin. The mother's hands in and out of washers,
her pocket of quarters swaying with her hips as she wheels
her clothes to the dryer, one hand still on the nape, one hand on the cart.
The clank of metal on metal, quarters dropping, the dryers revving to start.
Spinning washers. Whirr of dryers. Soda machine humming.
Baskets on hips, underneath chairs and tables. The infant
boy or girl, stretching out its arms, balls its hands, gazes
up at its mother's shoulders tensing as she shifts the carrier higher
on her chest and re-offers the orange. Its small mouth sucking her finger
and the orange as if there is no difference between them, its mouth and her finger,
its mouth and the orange. The mother swaying one leg to the other,
grabbing a skirt, then folding. The infant still strapped to her, whimpering
for the orange, hands pushing at her chest, her lean arms gently
placing the clothes in a basket. One last shift of carrier, she lines up the basket
on her hip, with the other leans on the door, hand on the infant's nape, swings it

open.

ornament

It just happened—
       my head
rammed into
the bathroom
          sink,
kneed a few
times in the kidney.
Gathering
myself, to not
think of
         fists
     on my skin,
gritting teeth
behind
them—my
         eye
      fat, red like
an ornament,
heavy as sleep.
Just twelve
        blocks
to get my story
straight,
        twelve
        blocks
until Mrs. Finley
     pulls me aside,
asking
why I didn't stay
        home.

The class
won't talk to my
lopsided

        face;
they just stare,
not having seen
the beating

    fourth-graders
get at my

        house—
where you learn
the stress

    of a pressman's
ink-caked hands.

    How simple
to climb
toys at recess
without a swollen

        eyebrow
    in my gaze.
To not know
the floors
and corners

    of my house
as I do
this morning,

        hands
raking my legs.

Firing a .38 at Age Sixteen

Pointing the barrel skyward,
  I squeezed the pistol's
trigger—small blast
    of gunpowder—after midnight
in McKinley Park. I stood
  near the dull glow of the park
fence under a streetlamp—
    my breath steaming in the frozen
diaper-stink air. I tried to hop
  over the fence and sprint
off into the knee-high thicket
    of dormant weeds, but my finger
caught one of the links.
  My legs straddling the fence,
I jerked the finger free
    but dropped the pistol
that was wedged in the small
  of my back. Had I left the .38
—in the dirt, the barrel
    glowing like oil
in a gutter puddle—some
  kid like me from the block
might have found the pistol
    and fired it off in a back
alley amid a circle of friends.
  But it was the first time
I'd heard gunpowder crack
    in my hands, sending a slug
into the winter-heavy night.
  So I picked up the pistol,
wiped it clean, and tucked
    it back in my waistline.

Randolph on Fire

All I could do was watch until his half-

                          whimper of fear

came to breath. Too brewed to know how his legs

                                 began roaring to blackness,

he could not find his face in the succession,

                            the utterance, not words—

a scream, a dance—the succession, running

in place, slapping

               his thighs, gasoline britches,

bursting near the chicken coop.

The yard birds ruffled and clucked,

                      white plumes flung in the air—

snow and flame and screaming—

                  the undazzle of fire.

cityscape

snow-caked   bottle in the gutter
snow-caked curb   snow-caked   boots
                          stomping
the concrete   half-smoked   butts
smashed into concrete cracks
a cream '79 cutlass leans its way around
the corner   sludge snow   overcast   damp
street   dull shine of a pistol   pedestrians
trudging   against the body seeping cold
a scattered crowd of bundled teenagers
fronting the bus bench on 23rd and Western
their breath steaming up the corner
                          one of them
dribbling a basketball   almost lyricizing
about his brother's   makeshift   condom
a bread sack and rubber band   the backdrop
a superette   bars bolted over the windows

crosstown

As the riders step out into the glum,

        deadbeat day, greasy, thick, and the dingy air

crawls from the door to my seat—I think

              of the time hands tightened around my throat

and face. I low from the off-white wall,

        my legs dangled, and he slung me to the floor.

I could not read it, the word that got me beaten

              and bloody. Sounding it out *ruh-ing*—

knocked upside my head for not knowing

        what I was spelling meant, *r-i-n-g*. I step

onto the grid, Western Avenue, where on either side

              of the street the guts of houses still stand,

rickety on their foundations.

Work 6 blocks, on the corner of McKinley,

        where inside I stack dishes, clean grease traps

and flip burgers. Two blocks, through an alley, craggy,

              shattered bottles of Mickey's, the smell of grease.

I see a mutt, its coat almost cinder-gray, mangy

        at the tail and neck, sniffing its way through a bag

of trash it must have gnawed open with its teeth.

              Mobbing out of the alley and onto NW 23rd,

a store—every window barred, folks out front,

        leaning up against the wall, paper-bagged bottles in hand.

I walk to a cooler of beer and find the tallest,

              cheapest can of malt. Rattle of change,

the beeping door, back out on 23rd.

Twilight, 90 degrees, some kids shirtless,
licking Red Bomber popsicles, ice-cream truck
        chiming its way up the block. As I make
my way through McKinley Park, I remember
    the time, amid an onslaught of lights,
the cops found a teenager in the parking-
        lot dumpster, shot through the dome.

How do I sound it out, even still, dreading
    a barrage of blows coming after every misread
word? How do I spell grease popping
        up from the grill and onto my face and hands?

On break, cigarette burning on my lips,
    wheeling a load of soggy-bagged trash
to the dumpster, reminds me that the bus driver
        said the victim was a kid that lived on 10th
and Kelly, and that the gunman is still a mystery.

Staggering the Sidewalk

It wasn't how I'd once seen it: hag-looking mamas
clacking their heels, the occasional twirl of the purse,
hands resting on their hips,

                      all of them lined up on the street—
made-up hair sprayed all sideways, goosing crotches,
pitching a tug.

          She was in her early
twenties and on her way out of a bar, wearing
a black-lace number, and unlike most nights—

                  usually walking
with a pink-faced man, her arms wrapped around his

                             waist,
thumb, maybe, hooked in a belt-loop—she was alone,
bangs falling in her eyes.

                Her dull, regal face,
lipstick smeared across her chin,
slurring out one-liners, ready to turn a trick.

It was not the humming nostrils, tinkle of a belt,
or a lonesome ache, remnants of a whiskey night—

not *her ticket to romantic places,*
alleys, beside a dumpster, lips shiny as butter,

                        it was habit
that sent her wandering for a companion,

                a daddy she'd lay
eyes on, jump-start, and dazzle.

Listo

Grass-matted face
    from having
        slept it off.
Aching at the joints,
    his bones crouched
        on the creek
            bank—
washing gold
    from his lips, shirt
sleeves, britches, fingers.
    He thinks about it
        every day,
the wheeze
    in his chest,
sounding as huffing
        ought to.
Tilt back the listo,
    cough it down,
sweat it out midday
        on a park
bench, can of Midas in hand,
        shining
    on the knee,
head bobbing—a dull,
        gold smile
    on his pursed lips.
        Listo
at daybreak, nightfall,
    noon, staggering
        in the alleys,
dragging his shoulder
    along dumpsters
and cinder-block walls,

huffing

and huffing—

his eye dead

in the socket, stabbed

with a fork

as he scurried

in a foggy

dawn for his brother's

last corner of listo.

Stepping heavy,

noon and nightfall,

cough it down,

sleep it off, listo

at daybreak,

huffing

and huffing until

there is no liver

or lung in him.

Caught fire.

Leg ran over.

Stitches along the

gut—

liver and lungs

of gold, lying

wherever he ends up.

Under a bridge.

Park bench. Ditches.

Rock

for pillow. His crouched

bones almost

popping out of his thinning

skin.

cityscape

clank and squeal clank and squeal in the street
heads calling for work   standing at the bus bench
heads   one of them   in a ripped coat and Thriller t-shirt
taking the last rip of a smoke   stomping the butt
into the concrete cracks   sludge snow   oil in a gutter
puddle   the superette opens its doors   winos
arms crossed into their pits   shuffle inside   emerge
paper-bagged   forties of Steel Reserve in hand
and shuffle off   into the snow-glowing alley

Sour Mash

Face down in the dirt yard, head gashed from a stumble—
    he climbed up from the ground, stinking and drunk, wet
        to the knee, and asked if Aunt Ida poured out his stash.
    If she had, he might have vanished, but the whiskey
was where he left it: shoved through a hole in the box spring.
    It was a fog-swept morning—water-limp leaves scattered
        on the street—he swayed in the flung rain and loosened
    the lid, swigged the Kentucky Deluxe down, then with a thick
sigh hazing his face, sent the warming drink bellyward.
    Two weeks out, he was shouting in dive watering
        holes, shooting stick, five dollars a rack, making
    attempts at necking any raspy-voiced booze-hag
he stumbled into. Now, lint pocketed, out on the trailer porch,
    blood-hardened ear, blood-caked hair, sour mash between his legs—
        his mumbling head; black, greasy nest of hair falling in his face.

Seasonal cityscape

kids licking popsicles
a row of dingy feet
shine in the sun

red leaves caught
against a steel fence
rain spattering and spattering

squirming
mud-caked boots
in the slush alley

wet-crotched
sockless   finger hooked
around a jug of night train

the bombed wall says 360°
below the aerosoled numbers
a skyline

10th Street Anthem

The city ends here. Dim-lit shacks

                    on the grid; in the feinting

light of evening a mother and son stand out on the sidewalk,

where the inklings

            of daylight are just enough that, with touch

and sight, she can slowly pluck each louse

                  from her son's head.

The mother's face,

          wrinkled, an unfolded pucker and smile,

her stringy, blonde hair dangling around her shoulders—

the son,

      chin to chest shirtless, staring at the sidewalk.

We, the onlookers on the corner,

              do not know shame,

chin to chest, Midas in the night,

           huffers

in the night, shirtless in the night that comes

down humid, streetlight that comes down platinum,

                 skin

in the streetlight, a pack of boys sprinting in the streetlight.

The city ends with bullet hole, ends with light bills,

              with welfare

and food stamps—we pluck and sprint, gulp down malt

and take it to the head—

        we huff the daylights out of our heads.

A pack of boys sprinting in the streetlight,

           barefoot and platinum

in the streetlight—a primered Skylark comes thumping

up the street on hubcaps, the driver's hoodie up,

                      elbow out

the window, the headliner coming down over his head

like a bedsheet.

                Beyond the dim guts of houses, beyond platinum,

beyond nothing ancient,

                          beyond the spine of civics, beyond the reach

of illuminated lots, beyond the reaching circuits—

                                it ends

with the spotty mutt, ends with some boney kid

                                  stashing his butterfly

blade in his tube sock, ends with a flock of winos huffing

Midas on a ramshackle porch, acting out their 20s and 30s

before the gash of scars, skill of fist,

                      before

the rusted shell of the tire factory was rusted—the last time

the potholed, divoted

                    asphalt smelled of hot rocks and tar.

A McDonald's cheeseburger wrapper

                        in the gutter.

Night Train bottle in the gutter. Diaper in the gutter.

Flattened mutt in the gutter. Barefoot

                      and platinum,

a pack of boys, sprinting

                off into the dumpster-stink alley.

Jack Move

We put in the lick on that dude with the Skylark
'cause the speakers in his trunk made the mutts bark.

Ducking along the street, parked cars, in shadow,
I pulled out the slimjim and shoved it down the window.

Taking too long, C.J. said, *don't make a sound.*
Double-O gonna swoop this corner any minute now.

I found the lock and jerked a few times, I hit the latch,
popped the trunk, unwired the speakers, C.J. snatched.

This dude's hooptie was foul, shit-green, primered fender,
sitting on some rusted hubcaps, blue bandana on the mirror.

With the loot in his arms, C.J. ran to his '84 Cutlass,
while I unscrewed the amp, ripped out the wires fast

as I could, 'cause I knew pigs liked to roll this block,
shining their lights, gripping their sticks, guns cocked.

C.J. rolled up beside me with the headlights off,
the window rolled down: *hurry up man, the fuckin' cops.*

I jumped in his ride, amp and wires still in my clutches.
He drove a few blocks away, and I sparked a Dutchie.

We gotta hock them speakers, they gonna shut off my lights,
my ass barely gets grub on the shit we do every night.

We rolled to Tran's on 23rd to get some booze, maybe a 5th,
but after we counted our ends, Ripple was all we could get.

Aerosol

solitude

The woman in the Levis poem, that gardenia, that voice whose face had been written
        about by another poet, *Ruined*,
she called it, that face, that voice sung with slight hum, a reverie she would have
        performed
in the smokiest spotlight—
a woman who could sound weeping into words.

Solitude she called: spring, bloom, early evening daydream,
a lover gone, the permanence of memory until her lover returned—an affair she
        sang a story to, her voice,
raspy, wet with whiskey.

There are photos: her lips, her teeth, muted—photos of her clinching into a
        microphone,
one eye shut, the other a glazed twinkle—it must have been a man's suit jacket she
        draped over her shoulder,
leaving one arm bare, softly lit in what looks to be a photo taken in a booth the two
        lovers could
have ambled into on a spring or autumn night.

No, I got it wrong—she sang for the tips and might have tucked her folded money
        somewhere
in that shoulderless lounge number she always seemed to be wearing. And she didn't
        sing of an affair
or a man, but of a brothel where affairs are acted out with whispers and promises,
        before and after sex,
and sometimes by appointment.

Ruined, no other word for it,

no other face, no song she sang to make it so, for it wasn't a song, it was a moan, a

      brothel noise,

a pitiless echo of the ruined.

That echo. That fruit.

She must have known, years later, dying in a hospital was the same as dying in a

      brothel.

The same lynching. The same rope.

The Robbery

Red ambulance flicker, curbstone, wheels, a gurney. Down the breezeway a baby,
    crying out among the gawk-mouthed heads.
Knifed, sliced, the man bleeding through the gauze and onto his belly.

It reminds me of the night when my mother and I slept in our LTD while the cops
    surrounded our apartment complex.
I remember someone standing near the yellow tape saying 2A had robbed the market
    across the street, that the manager was shot twice—
once in the arm, once in the shoulder—and that the gunmen were held up in their
    apartment, squealing threats from their window.

When I think of it now, the danger, the eventual gunshots echoing off gray brick, I
    remember the panicked yells of inquiry,
a girl crying her daddy was shot.

But the knifed man, now under gauze and tubing, hadn't robbed a store, and the
    baby, now on its mother's hip, was quiet and drooling.

When the cops searched 2A, they found money stuffed in the couches, in pots and
pans, in the pages of storybooks, and as each officer, one by one, emerged from the
    apartment holding pistols and rifles, my mother told me to go back to sleep.

I don't remember her carrying me to my bed, only waking the next day when the
    girl who cried *daddy*,
knocked at our door, asked if I could come out and play.

Now when I look at her, that same girl, with a busted eye and lip, I wonder: if when
she stabbed was she stabbing the boyfriend who beat her for burning supper or was
it her dad for wrenching his arm around her neck, prodding a pistol at her head on
    that balmy night of echo and threat.

For a second I think of asking her, "Whatever happened to your dad? Is he still in jail?"

But I realize it may not even be the same girl, though I want it to be.

For some reason I think if she kills that man, if he bleeds to death before the
        ambulance can make it to the hospital,
somehow the brief triumph of metal over flesh would rid my memory of the deafening
        crack of gunpowder, and its long shout in the night.

Stranded

There he was puffing his way toward
me, smoke at his lips and out the nostrils;
his face scrunched under a potato-chip hat,
　shirt hanging from his shoulders sweat
　　　　　　　　　　　　　heavy.
Behind him a constellation of workers
crouched near the strawberry vines in their
wide-brimmed hats; one woman had a baby,
　sheet-wrapped to her back, and a teenaged
　　　　　　　　　　　　girl
walked the field rows, barefoot, with a pail
and dipper of water. Behind me sat my lemon,
overheated and parked in the knee-high grass,
　the hood propped up. *No habla español,*
　　　　　　　　　　　I said,
hand over my brow, the other in my pocket.
No one spoke English, but as we walked
toward shade and I was offered water, I knew
　to drink, and hours later when offered
　　　　　　　　　　　　tortillas,
pinto beans, and potatoes, I knew to eat. As
the bright day gave way to sounds of cicadas
and the reddening set of the sun, the man
　approached me again and led me to his
　　　　　　　　　　　truck.
And driving to the nearest town, he talked
to me, pointing to the fields on either side
of the road, and I knew then he was talking
　of work, and the long, slow days picking fruit.

Eating against a Wall

She rolled out the bamboo mat
near a brick wall

          as her husband hoisted
a gallon milk jug to his lips

               to gulp down water.

Then, with their lank arms draped
over their raised knees—
chopsticks in one hand, Cool Whip bowl in the other,
heads slumped—

          they tugged
at clumps of noodles,

            slurping them up.

Though I didn't think of it then,

               it was the first
time I'd seen someone eat with sticks.

I peered out from my seat on the bus,
thinking that eating

          had never been so

               transient,
that somehow we all end up here,

             displaced,

documented.

An Aerosoled Representation of the Maya and Moché

It stank in the ground nooks, pissed on by drunken, fumbling passersby—the mural

under a streetlight that revealed rust-reds, ear adornments, aerosoled slope of
forehead—

werejaguars in tow, half-morphed, under the dazzling Huaca Del Sol—the eroding,
cracking mural
that at one time reached the limits of the building's masonry.

I stood at the mural, hands in my pockets, unsure if we would ever touch again,

not because the next day I would have to leave you suddenly—head resting in your
palm, cigarette lit
and wedged between your fingers, gradually blowing smoke from your lips and out of
your third-floor window—

it was because, as we looked upon the mural, you said,
it's just paint, your face expressionless as if it was just another moment.

What it was, was a block corner—the other side of the wall, Garcia's Grocery.
As we walked through the entrance on either side, we saw crates of mangoes and
gala apples stacked into pyramids, the owner's daughter, polishing each fruit in her
small brown hand.

Even then, shopping for beer, I knew you had seen more than just paint on that
fading wall, and after we left the store, walking through the Mission, I tried not to
question you, to ruin our last hours together.

And had I known we were not going to speak for years, I might have said nothing,
      just walked silently,
like the time I woke up on a park bench, years before we met.
I stepped heavy through McKinley Park, my lip and eye still puffy from the scuffle,
      the autumn light
stringing, already cold and distant, through the bare-limbed trees.

———

I was fifteen, six hours homeless, and no, it wasn't the first time I'd slept on a park bench.

I spent the day filling out applications at fast-food joints and diners, wherever I thought
      I could get a meal.

Josie's is where I ended up. Piling plate after plate, my hands waterlogged and
      scalded.
The dishwasher had not shown up that day, and despite my patchy and bruised face,
      the manager tossed me an apron.

Had you wanted me to stay, I might have seen that mural a few more times before
Garcia's was sold, the wall painted; and if I had a chance to walk that block again
      with you, I would say muralists are the translators of dreams.

As I waited in line at the Oakland Greyhound terminal to board the bus—one
hand, bag in tow, the other, my ticket—a mother in front of me shifted her
daughter higher on her hip. The girl, snot-faced, began to bawl, and with the
      slightest roll of the tongue the mother began to lull her to sleep.

———

A day later, I stood behind her, reboarding the bus, under a flicker of light, late night,
      Amarillo and the greasy sweat of July.
Workers scurried about, pushing carts, wielding gas pumps, stuffing bags in the
      bus's belly.

She handed her ticket to the driver—traveling east, through Tennessee.

I watched as she settled in her seat by a window.

Later I woke to Arkansas fog, thick like cotton along the trunks of poplars—
mother and daughter across the aisle, coiled up in a jacket, asleep since Oklahoma.

The bus revved its way through morning—she rose to the window, the bead of her eye
    scanned the damp landscape.

I wondered who had sent her away on those slow travels, half-beaten, wearing a man's
    jacket.

She stared at her daughter, maybe wondering if she will carry her hips.

It was 1999. Fort Smith, and I had already changed buses. All points north: St. Louis,
    Davenport, Chicago.

The bus swayed as the driver backed us out of the terminal—she was on the phone, her
    daughter asleep on her shrugged hip.

————

Our last night together, we stumbled down the street—lit on margaritas, and on
    the way home stopped into
Garcia's for more beer—I remember the block corner, filled with yells and laughter
    from the bar next door.

With the sack of bottles in my arms, I told you how the night air smelt of tar and
    exhaust, how me leaving
the next day meant I might not come back. It was like the moment when two
    strangers find each other,

say what they must in the dim lounge light, leave together, and the next day say
what they must out of shame.

But we had known each other for years, and I began to realize you already knew
and had left me before that night in The Mission.

And just like that night in McKinley Park, wandering the pathways for the quietest
bench untouched by the autumn wind,
you went back to your flat, and I walked the blocks thinking of what to say that
next morning—stuffing my bags quietly, shamed I owed you rent.

As the reddening dawn began to thin, the sunlight settled into the otherwise dark
nooks of buildings, and strayed into your window.
Towing my bag, I pulled the door shut, and as I walked down the hallway, I heard
you latch the lock.

———

Years later, when you called after midnight, your voice hoarser since we last spoke,

we argued, and again I was ashamed, and if you had asked, "Do you still?" I would
have said, *yes.*
But you didn't and instead told me that just months after we'd split you'd had a daughter.

A week later I was bound away on the Greyhound. All points west. And as the bus
pulled off Route 66 and into the Flagstaff terminal,
I peered from my window seat and saw you with a toddler in your arms.

As I stepped off the bus, you were standing there, your hip shrugged to the right,
propping the toddler up.
I remember a tiny, round face, sticky, a hand knuckled around a lollipop. I remember a
face half my own.

Acknowledgments

Humble thanks to the editors and readers of the following journals

for originally publishing my poems:

American Poet: "Root Juice."

Many Mountains Moving: "Bluetop."

Narrative Magazine: "Gunshot Conjure," "One-Room Apartment."

Oregon Literary Review: "Sour Mash," "Solitude," "Randolph on Fire," "Staggering the Sidewalk."

The Ontario Review: "The Carnival," "Hunter's Moon," "Mama's Work," "Pickax."

Third Coast: "Eating against a Wall," "An Aerosoled Representation of the Maya and Moché."

To Topos: "Coin Laundry," "Crosstown," "Nick Cheater."

Deepest gratitude to my teachers Jon Davis and Arthur Sze for their dedication and guidance; to my mother, Sherry England; to my brother, Kevin Frazier; to Sherwin Bitsui, Shane Book, and Orlando White for their thoughts and vision; to the Institute of American Indian Arts; finally, to my wife, Summer, and our two children, Karis and Kenji, as we grow and learn from one another.

About the Author

Santee Frazier is a citizen of the Cherokee Nation of Oklahoma. He holds a BFA from the Institute of American Indian Arts and an MFA from Syracuse University. His work has appeared in *American Poet, Ontario Review,* and various other literary journals. He currently lives in Syracuse, New York, with his wife and two children.

Library of Congress Cataloging-in-Publication Data

Frazier, Santee, 1978–
   Dark thirty / Santee Frazier.
      p. cm. — (Sun tracks ; v. 65)
      ISBN 978-0-8165-2814-1 (pbk. : acid-free paper)
      1. Cherokee Indians—Poetry. 2. Indians of North
America—Poetry. I. Title.
PS3606.R429D37   2009
811'.6—dc22   2008033644